# ad🍎m sense

## The CRACR Blueprint Journal

A companion journal for teachers engaging with the CRACR model

## CHAOS TO CALM CLASSROOMS
## THE CRACR BLUEPRINT

# BY MICHELE ADAMSON

Published in Australia by Michele Adamson

First published in Australia 2026
This edition published 2026



Cover design, typesetting: WorkingType (www.workingtype.com.au)



ISBN: 978-1-7645640-2-1

**Adamsense**

michele@adamsense.com

Quantity sales, Special discounts are available on quantity purchases by corporations, associations, and others.  For details, contact the publisher at the address above.

## How to Use This Journal

This journal is a space just for you. It's not assessed, marked, or shared - it's an honest reflection tool to help you deepen your practice and make meaningful changes in your teaching.

Each section encourages you to consider key questions aligned with the CRACR model. Writing your thoughts down will help clarify what's working, where you're stuck, and how to move forward with confidence and care.

## A Moment to Pause

You'll find colouring pages integrated throughout this journal. They are not just decorative; they are intentional. Reflecting on behaviour leadership requires a regulated nervous system. When we are calm, we think clearly. When we think clearly, we respond purposefully. Colouring is a simple yet powerful way to support that regulation.

## Why Colouring Works

When teachers colour:

- Heart rate slows

- Cognitive overload reduces

- Emotional reactivity decreases

- Reflective thinking strengthens

It creates space.

- Space between stimulus and response.

- Space between frustration and clarity.

- Space to reflect before reacting.

Use these pages as reset moments.

Not as another task but as permission to pause.

Calm leaders build calm classrooms.

Be honest, be specific, and be kind to yourself. Growth begins with reflection.

# Contents

# CHAPTER 1

# Knowing yourself as a teacher

## Part One - Who Are You?

Take a few moments to write freely. Let your thoughts flow without judgement.

Describe yourself as a teacher in three words.

_______________________________________________

Why did you choose those words?

Write here:

_______________________________________________

_______________________________________________

_______________________________________________

What brought you into teaching in the first place?

Is that reason still driving you today?

Write here:

_______________________________________________

_______________________________________________

_______________________________________________

What values do you hold when it comes to working with young people?
How do those values show up in your classroom?

Write here:

_______________________________________________

_______________________________________________

_______________________________________________

_______________________________________________

# Part Two – What Are You Struggling With?

Be honest with yourself. This is for your eyes only.

What is your biggest current struggle when it comes to student behaviour?
Try to be specific. Is it one student? A class dynamic? A lack of support?

Write here:

_______________________________________________

_______________________________________________

_______________________________________________

_______________________________________________

_______________________________________________

_______________________________________________

How does this challenge make you feel, emotionally and professionally?

Write here:

___________________________________________

___________________________________________

___________________________________________

___________________________________________

___________________________________________

___________________________________________

On a scale of 1–10, how confident do you feel managing behaviour in your classroom? What would help you move just one number higher?

Confidence rating:        / 10

To move higher, I could:

___________________________________________

___________________________________________

___________________________________________

___________________________________________

___________________________________________

___________________________________________

___________________________________________

# FROM CHAOS TO CALM

*As you colour, consider: What has shifted in me this term?*

# Part Three – What Do You Want?

Clarify your intentions for this journey.

Why are you reading this book?
What are you hoping to learn or change?

Write here:

_______________________________________________

_______________________________________________

_______________________________________________

_______________________________________________

What would success look like by the end of this book?
Picture your ideal classroom. What's happening? How do you feel in it?

Write here:

_______________________________________________

_______________________________________________

_______________________________________________

_______________________________________________

_______________________________________________

# Part Four – What's Standing in Your Way?

This is your space to get real about the roadblocks.

What internal or external obstacles are preventing you from achieving the classroom you want?
(Think about mindset, time, student dynamics, school systems, support, etc.)

Write here:

_______________________________________________

_______________________________________________

_______________________________________________

_______________________________________________

_______________________________________________

# Part Five – Where To Next?

Now let's take one small step forward.

What's one small but intentional action you could take this week
to improve behaviour management or your own wellbeing in the classroom?

Write here:

_______________________________________________

_______________________________________________

_______________________________________________

---

What support or resources do you need to take that next step confidently?

Write here:

---

---

---

---

---

---

# Final Thought

Growth doesn't happen all at once. It begins with awareness, followed by consistent, compassionate action. Keep returning to this journal as you read the book and use your reflections to shape your next steps with clarity and purpose.

**You've got this.**

# CHAPTER 2

# The Functions of Behaviour

## Attention-Seeking Behaviour

Some students seek connection in ways that can be challenging, by calling out, interrupting, creating disruptions, or constantly seeking reassurance. These behaviours are often signals, not defiance.

Use the prompts below to reflect on your own experiences with attention-seeking behaviour in your classroom.

### Reflective Prompts

1. **What specific attention-seeking behaviours have you observed in a student or group of students?**

Be as specific as possible. Think about both subtle and overt behaviours.

*Write here:*

_______________________________________________

_______________________________________________

_______________________________________________

_______________________________________________

2.  **How do you typically respond to these behaviours?
    Consider your instinctive reactions and any patterns in your
    responses.**

*Write here:*

_______________________________________________________________

_______________________________________________________________

_______________________________________________________________

_______________________________________________________________

3.  **Which responses seem to have a positive effect, and which ones
    don't appear to work?
    Reflect on what escalates the behaviour versus what calms or
    redirects it.**

*Write here:*

_______________________________________________________________

_______________________________________________________________

_______________________________________________________________

_______________________________________________________________

4.  **What could you do differently to encourage more positive behaviour
    and build connection?**

Think about proactive strategies, consistent responses, or alternative ways to
provide attention.

*Write here:*

_______________________________________________________________

_______________________________________________________________

_______________________________________________________________

**Reminder:**

This journal is a space for honest reflection, not judgement. The goal is to explore new strategies that foster connection, clarity, and change. Behaviour is communication. When we listen with curiosity, we give ourselves the chance to respond with purpose.

# Escape Behaviour

Some students respond to challenge or discomfort by avoiding tasks, withdrawing, or acting out in ways that remove them from the situation. These behaviours often signal anxiety, frustration, or a lack of confidence.

This reflection will help you better understand these patterns and explore ways to support engagement and success.

## Reflective Prompts

1. **Can you identify a student who shows signs of escape behaviour?** What specific behaviours have you noticed? Are they task-avoidant, emotionally withdrawn, or using disruption to avoid demands?

*Write here:*

_______________________________________________

_______________________________________________

_______________________________________________

_______________________________________________

_______________________________________________

_______________________________________________

## 2. How have you been responding to this behaviour?

What strategies or reactions do you tend to use in the moment?

*Write here:*

## 3. Has your approach been effective?

Why do you think it has or hasn't worked? What feedback, direct or indirect, have you noticed from the student?

*Write here:*

**4. What alternative strategies could you try to help this student stay engaged and feel more successful?**
Consider ways to adjust tasks, increase support, reduce overwhelm or build confidence.

*Write here:*

_______________________________________________

_______________________________________________

_______________________________________________

_______________________________________________

_______________________________________________

_______________________________________________

**Gentle Reminder:**

Escape behaviour is often a response to feeling unsafe, overwhelmed, or out of control. When we respond with curiosity rather than control, we open the door to connection, trust and more effective learning.

# FUNCTIONS OF BEHAVIOUR

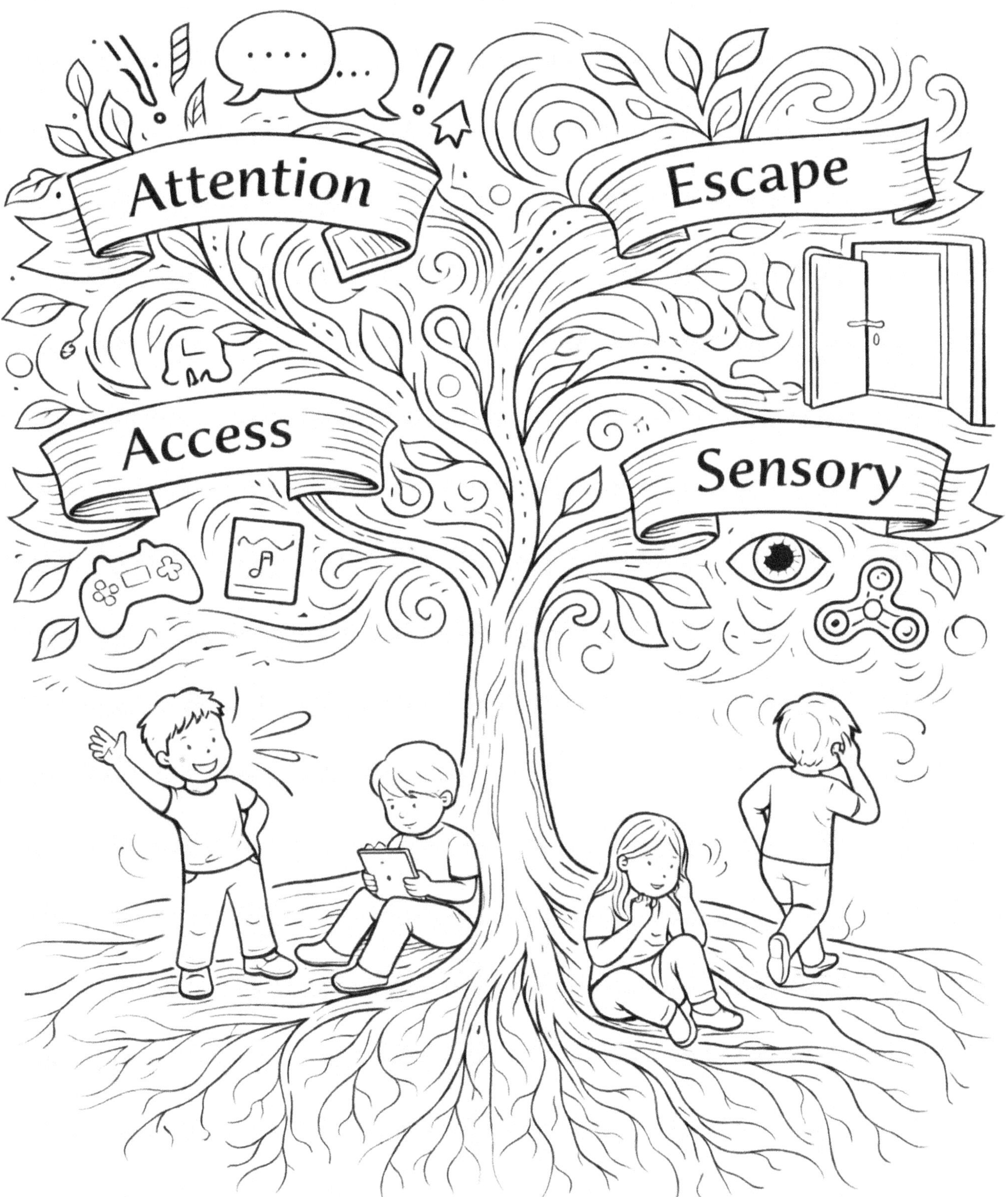


*As you colour, consider: What function might drive this behaviour?*

# Access-Seeking Behaviour

Some students act out not to avoid something but to *gain* something: attention, help, a preferred activity, or even a physical object. These behaviours can be subtle or disruptive, and our responses can unintentionally reinforce them if we're not careful.

Use the following prompts to guide your reflection:

## 1.  Spot the Behaviour

**What access-seeking behaviours have you observed in your classroom?**
Think about students who frequently call out, hover at your desk, interrupt others, or create distractions to gain your attention or access to something they want.

*Write here:*

_______________________________________________

_______________________________________________

_______________________________________________

_______________________________________________

## 2.  Unintentional Reinforcement

**Have there been times when you may have unintentionally reinforced access-seeking behaviour?**
Reflect on how your responses, like giving in, offering help too quickly, or providing attention during the behaviour, might have sent mixed signals.

*Write here:*

_______________________________________________

_______________________________________________

## 3.   What's the Student Really Seeking?

**When you look deeper, what is the student *actually* trying to gain?**
Is it a connection? Reassurance? Access to materials? Time with a preferred peer or adult? Identifying the true motivator helps you respond more effectively.

*Write here:*

## 4. Plan a Positive Replacement Strategy

**What more appropriate way could the student use to get what they need, and how can you support that?**
Think about how you might teach or reinforce a more positive behaviour (e.g., raising a hand, using a help card, waiting patiently).

*Write here:*

# Sensory Function of Behaviour

## Seeing Regulation, Not Disruption

Before reacting to behaviour, we must ask:
Is this behaviour fulfilling a sensory need?

Some behaviours are not about attention, avoidance or power.
They are about regulation.

Use the reflections below to deepen your understanding.

## 1.  Noticing Patterns

Think about a student who frequently:

- Taps, rocks, hums or fidgets

- Struggles to sit still

- Covers ears or avoids bright light

- Seeks movement or pressure

**Describe the Behaviour**

What does it look like? *Write here:*

_______________________________________________

_______________________________________________

When does it tend to occur?

☐  During quiet work

☐  During transitions

☐  After lunch

☐   When stressed

☐   When bored

☐   During group work

☐   Other:

___

What patterns do you notice?

___

___

___

## 2.  Shifting your lens

Initially, how did you interpret this behaviour?

☐   Disrespectful

☐   Deliberate disruption

☐   Attention-seeking

☐   Lack of effort

☐   "Just being silly"

☐   Other:

___

Now consider:

Could this behaviour be sensory regulation?

What might the student be trying to feel?

☐ Calmer

☐ More alert

☐ Less overwhelmed

☐ More grounded

☐ Less anxious

☐ Other:

Explain your thinking. *Write here*:

## 3.  **Your response check**

How have you responded in the past?

☐ Verbal warning

☐ Consequence

☐ Seat change

☐ Ignored it

☐ Asked them to "stop"

☐ Other:

Did your response support regulation or suppress it?

_______________________________________________

_______________________________________________

## 4.  Proactive Strategies

If this behaviour is sensory-driven, what could you try instead?

- ☐ Movement breaks

- ☐ Flexible seating

- ☐ Wobble cushion

- ☐ Fidget tool

- ☐ Quiet corner

- ☐ Headphones

- ☐ Scheduled regulation time

- ☐ Visual cue

- ☐ Collaboration with support staff

Write one strategy you will trial:

_______________________________________________

How will you explain this support to the class to promote empathy?

_______________________________________________

_______________________________________________

_______________________________________________

# CASE STUDY REFLECTION

Think about the Liam scenario.

If you were his teacher:

What would your first reaction have been?

_______________________________________________________

What would your regulated, informed response be?

_______________________________________________________

_______________________________________________________

Complete this sentence:

"When I see sensory behaviour, instead of assuming _____________________,

I will consider _____________________________________."

## Now, let's bring it all together. Do we have a clearer understanding of the Functions of Behaviour?

This chapter introduced you to the four key functions of student behaviour: attention, escape, access, and sensory. Understanding why students behave in certain ways enables you to respond with more clarity, purpose, and care.

Use the activities below to reflect on your classroom and make meaningful links between theory and practice.

## Journal Activity

Take a few quiet moments to reflect and write freely in response to the following prompts:

1. **Have you ever misunderstood a student's sensory-seeking behaviour as deliberate disruption?**

   How did you respond at the time, and how might you respond differently now?

   *Write here:*

   ___________________________________________

   ___________________________________________

   ___________________________________________

   ___________________________________________

2. **What small changes could you make in your classroom to better support students with sensory needs?**

   *Write here:*

   ___________________________________________

   ___________________________________________

   ___________________________________________

   ___________________________________________

3.  **Looking back over the chapter, what have you learned about the functions of behaviour?**

    How do these functions - **attention**, **escape**, **access**, and **sensory** - show up in your classroom?

    *Write here:*

**4. Can you now identify the likely function behind some of the challenging behaviours you've encountered?**

What patterns are beginning to emerge in your observations?

*Write here:*

---

---

---

---

---

---

---

---

## Moving from Reaction to Clarity 

Behaviour is communication.

Before we correct it, we must understand it.

## Brainstorm Activity: What Might This Look Like in Your Classroom?

Complete the table below.

## Step 1: Identify the Function

Use the table below to record behaviours you've observed and think about what function they might serve.

| Attention | Escape | Access | Sensory |
|---|---|---|---|
| What I saw? | What I saw? | What I saw? | What I saw? |
| How have I typically responded to these behaviours? | How have I typically responded to these behaviours? | How have I typically responded to these behaviours? | How have I typically responded to these behaviours? |
| Were my responses reinforcing the behaviour or redirecting it? | Were my responses reinforcing the behaviour or redirecting it? | Were my responses reinforcing the behaviour or redirecting it? | Were my responses reinforcing the behaviour or redirecting it? |

| Attention | Escape | Access | Sensory |
|---|---|---|---|
| What could I do differently now that I better understand the why? | What could I do differently now that I better understand the why? | What could I do differently now that I better understand the why? | What could I do differently now that I better understand the why? |

Examples to guide thinking (not to copy, just to spark reflection):

- Calling out
- Avoiding work
- Refusing transitions
- Fidgeting
- Arguing
- Leaving seat
- Emotional outbursts
- Distracting peers

This activity aims to help you link theory with your daily practice. Keep this table as a reference and revisit it regularly as you develop confidence and skills in behaviour management.

## A little reminder

- Not every behaviour is defiance.
- Some behaviours are communication.
- Some behaviours are regulation.
- When we shift from control to curiosity,
- We move from reaction to support.

# Chapter 3

# Caring

## Caring Relationships Improve Behaviour

### Journal Reflection: Reconnecting with a Challenging Student

Every teacher has encountered a student who pushes their limits, who drains energy, sparks frustration, or even makes us question our own effectiveness. But behind every behaviour is a story, and behind every story is a child who needs understanding.

This activity is not about blame or guilt. It's about honestly exploring the relationship between you and a student who has been difficult to connect with and beginning the process of rebuilding that connection.

### Step 1: Reflect Individually

Choose one student who has come to mind during this chapter - someone who causes you the most grief, frustration, or emotional exhaustion.

Answer the following questions honestly. There's no judgement here, just real talk and self-awareness.

**STUDENT'S NAME**

1.  **Do I genuinely care about this student? (Yes or No)**
    Be honest. Maybe you did once, but the daily grind has taken a toll.
    Where does your care for this child sit right now?

    *Write here:*

2.  **What does this student do – or not do – that makes me feel this way?**
    List the behaviours that frustrate or trigger you the most. Be specific
    and honest.

    *Write here:*

3.  **Can I think of one thing I like about this student?**
    If this feels difficult, pause and sit with the question. Look deeper.
    Try to find just one quality, habit, or strength, no matter how small.

    *Write here:*

**4. What might be blocking me from caring?**

Is it burnout? A repeated pattern? The student's home life?
Prior experiences or broken trust?

*Write here:*

---

---

---

**4. How can I begin to overcome this blockage?**

What mindset shift, support, or small action might help you reconnect with
this student in a more compassionate and productive way?

*Write here:*

---

---

---

# Final Thought:

Caring doesn't mean excusing poor behaviour; it means committing to respond
with intention, empathy, and boundaries. When you reconnect with your "why" and
your students' humanity, even the toughest relationships can begin to change.

As you colour, consider: What function might drive this behaviour?

# Chapter 4

# Rapport

## RAPPORT BUILDING: START WITH YOUR STORY

### Why This Matters

Let's take a moment to reflect on your own school experience. Our experiences as students shape who we are today as teachers. The way we were spoken to, supported, corrected, encouraged, or overlooked influences how we connect with students now, sometimes without us even realising it. When we understand our story, we can build rapport with intention rather than habit.

### REFLECTION TASK

### Think About Your Favourite Teacher

Think about a teacher you respected, enjoyed learning from, and maybe still think about today.

This might have been:

- A primary school teacher

- A high school teacher

- A coach

- A tutor

Take your time. Be honest. Write freely.

1. Who was the teacher? What made them memorable?

2. What did they do to build a connection with you?

3. How did that relationship affect your behaviour or motivation?

## 4. Did their rapport make a difference to your learning? How?

_______________________________________________

_______________________________________________

_______________________________________________

_______________________________________________

## 🍎 TURNING REFLECTION INTO PRACTICE

Read back over what you've written.

What patterns do you notice?

## Which qualities showed up?

☐ Warmth

☐ Fairness

☐ Humour

☐ High expectations

☐ Calmness

☐ Consistency

☐ Trust

☐ Listening

☐ Encouragement

☐ Patience

☐ Not giving up on you

☐ Other:

_______________________________________________

The biggest thing I realised from my own experiences with my teachers is:

_______________________________________________

_______________________________________________

_______________________________________________

_______________________________________________

One small rapport-building action I can try this week:

_______________________________________________

_______________________________________________

_______________________________________________

One student I want to intentionally build stronger rapport with:

_______________________________________________

_______________________________________________

_______________________________________________

How I will show them they matter (specific action):

______________________________________________

______________________________________________

______________________________________________

______________________________________________

______________________________________________

### Remember

Rapport is not about being liked.

It is about being consistent, safe, and steady.

When students feel seen and respected, behaviour shifts.

When behaviour shifts, learning follows.

And that begins with us.

Chapter 5

# Applying Boundaries

## SETTING BOUNDARIES: CLARITY CREATES SAFETY

### Let's Practise Setting Boundaries

Clear, purposeful boundaries are not about control; they are about establishing safety, predictability, and shared responsibility.

Let's take a moment to practise what setting clear, intentional boundaries looks like, just as you would in your own classroom.

### YOUR TASK

#### Step 1: Identify Your Core Expectations

On your own, write down **3–5 expectations** you believe are essential for a productive and respectful learning environment.

Examples might include:

- Devices away

- Active listening

- One voice at a time

- Participation encouraged

- Respectful language

## Write your 3 – 5 Essential Expectations below:

### 1. Why is this expectation important?

_______________________________________________________________

_______________________________________________________________

_______________________________________________________________

_______________________________________________________________

What would be a fair consequence if it isn't followed?

_______________________________________________________________

_______________________________________________________________

_______________________________________________________________

_______________________________________________________________

How would I explain this expectation to my students?

_______________________________________________________________

_______________________________________________________________

_______________________________________________________________

_______________________________________________________________

## 2. Why is this expectation important?

What would be a fair consequence if it isn't followed?

How would I explain this expectation to my students?

## 3. Why is this expectation important?

What would be a fair consequence if it isn't followed?

_______________________________________________

_______________________________________________

_______________________________________________

_______________________________________________

_______________________________________________

How would I explain this expectation to my students?

_______________________________________________

_______________________________________________

_______________________________________________

_______________________________________________

_______________________________________________

## 🍎 REFLECTION: ARE MY BOUNDARIES CLEAR?

Once complete, read back through your list and ask yourself:

- [ ] Are these expectations clear and specific?

- [ ] Would my students understand and buy into these?

- [ ] Have I included both the "what" and the "why"?

- [ ] Are the consequences fair, predictable, and consistent?

- [ ] Do these boundaries protect learning, not just control behaviour?

Write one insight you noticed:

_______________________________________________

_______________________________________________

_______________________________________________

_______________________________________________

## Accountability Statement

"If someone doesn't follow the agreed expectations, it's not your fault; it's their responsibility."

This is the accountability we want to build in our classrooms.

Boundaries are not personal. They are professional.

Keep this in mind as you reflect on how you will introduce, model, and consistently uphold boundaries in your teaching practice.

Clarity reduces chaos.

Consistency builds trust.

Trust strengthens learning.

Chapter 6

# Consequences

## CONSEQUENCES: TEACHING RESPONSIBILITY, NOT PUNISHMENT

### Why Consequences Matter

Consequences help students understand that every action has a positive or negative outcome. This isn't about punishment; it's about building responsibility, accountability, and self-regulation.

When consequences are clear, fair, and consistently applied, students feel safe. When they are unclear or inconsistent, confusion and frustration grow.

This reflection will help you examine your own beliefs and delivery around consequences.

### My beliefs about consequences

Take a moment to reflect honestly.

1.  **When I think about giving consequences, I feel:**

_______________________________________________

_______________________________________________

_______________________________________________

_______________________________________________

2.  **When I was growing up, how were consequences handled at home and at school, and what typically happened when a student made a poor choice?**

\
\
\
\
\

3.  **How might those experiences influence how I respond to student behaviour now?**

\
\
\
\

# CONSEQUENCES
## *Reflection*

As you colour, consider: What does my choice ripple outwards?

# CLEAR VS UNCLEAR CONSEQUENCES

Think about a time when a classroom (yours or someone else's) felt chaotic.

What was missing?

- [ ] Clear expectations
- [ ] Agreed consequences
- [ ] Consistent follow-through
- [ ] Calm delivery
- [ ] Student accountability
- [ ] Other:

_______________________________________________

What impact did that have on learning? What did you see unfold?

_______________________________________________

_______________________________________________

_______________________________________________

Now reflect on a classroom that felt structured and calm.

What role did consequences play?

_______________________________________________

_______________________________________________

_______________________________________________

# BUILDING MY CONSEQUENCE FRAMEWORK

Consequences should be fair, balanced, and foreseeable.

Choose one common behaviour challenge in your classroom.

Behaviour:

_______________________________________________

What is the related expectation?

_______________________________________________

What would be a logical, fair consequence?

_______________________________________________

How will I deliver it calmly and clearly?

_______________________________________________

How will I reinforce positive choices in this area?

_______________________________________________

_______________________________________________

_______________________________________________

# CALM DELIVERY CHECK

Read the following statement:

"If someone doesn't follow the agreed expectations, it's not my fault; it's their responsibility."

How comfortable am I separating behaviour from emotion?

☐   Very comfortable

☐   Somewhat comfortable

☐   I find this difficult

☐   I often take it personally

What helps me stay calm when behaviour escalates?

_______________________________________________

_______________________________________________

_______________________________________________

What is one phrase I can use to maintain calm authority?

Example: "You're choosing to ignore the agreement. This is the next step."

My phrase:

_______________________________________________

_______________________________________________

_______________________________________________

# EQUITY OVER EQUALITY

"Fair doesn't mean everyone gets the same. Fair means everyone gets what they need."

Think about a student who may require a differentiated response.

Who are they?

_______________________________________________

What support might they need?

___________________________________________________________

How can I explain fairness to the class in a way that builds understanding rather than resentment?

___________________________________________________________

___________________________________________________________

___________________________________________________________

## POWER STRUGGLE SELF-CHECK

When a student refuses a consequence, I tend to:

- [ ] Raise my voice

- [ ] Repeat myself

- [ ] Argue

- [ ] Walk away

- [ ] Offer a choice

- [ ] Stay calm and neutral

What would offering a choice sound like in my classroom?

___________________________________________________________

___________________________________________________________

___________________________________________________________

# Final Reflection

Clear consequences restore structure. Calm delivery protects rapport. Consistency builds trust.

What is one commitment I will make about consequences in my classroom moving forward?

## You are allowed to reset

Chapter 7

# Reflection

## TAKING STOCK OF YOUR PRACTICE

## Pause. Breathe. Reflect.

Reflection is where growth begins.

Take a few quiet minutes to sit with your thoughts and reflect on a recent classroom moment that challenged you. This could be a behaviour incident, a tough day, or a moment that left you feeling drained, frustrated, or unsure.

This is not about judgement. It is about clarity.

_______________________________________________

_______________________________________________

_______________________________________________

_______________________________________________

### Describe the Situation

What happened? Who was involved? What was the behaviour and how did you respond?

_______________________________________________

_______________________________________________

_______________________________________________

_______________________________________________

_______________________________________________

## How Did You Feel?

Be honest.

Were you frustrated, angry, helpless, overwhelmed, embarrassed, indifferent, or exhausted?

_______________________________________________

_______________________________________________

_______________________________________________

## What Was Your Instinctive Reaction?

Did you:

- ☐ Raise your voice

- ☐ Ignore the behaviour

- ☐ Follow your consequence steps

- ☐ Withdraw emotionally

- ☐ Seek support

- ☐ Stay calm and measured

- ☐ Other:

_______________________________________________

What did that reaction communicate to your students?

____________________________________________________________

____________________________________________________________

____________________________________________________________

## What Worked Well?

Is there anything you're proud of or would intentionally repeat?

____________________________________________________________

____________________________________________________________

____________________________________________________________

## What Could Have Been Done Differently?

If you could hit "rewind," how might you handle it with more clarity, calm or connection?

____________________________________________________________

____________________________________________________________

____________________________________________________________

## What Did This Reveal About Your Behaviour Management Approach?

Are there gaps? Are you responding consistently? Do you feel calm and in control? Are your expectations and consequences clear?

____________________________________________________________

## What Support or Strategy Might Help Next Time?

Think practically.

Do you need:

- [ ] A conversation with a colleague

- [ ] Clearer boundaries

- [ ] More consistent follow-through

- [ ] Time to regulate yourself

- [ ] A reset plan for that student

- [ ] A clearer script

- [ ] Leadership support

- [ ] Other:

Write one helpful support or strategy you will seek or implement:

## One Small Action for Tomorrow

Keep it simple and achievable.

What is one thing you will try, adjust or strengthen tomorrow?

# Final Thought

Reflection isn't about being hard on yourself. It's about recognising that every moment, especially the hard ones, carries insight.

The goal is progress, not perfection.

Growth happens when we pause, notice, and adjust.

If you feel comfortable, journal your responses in more detail or share one insight with a trusted colleague.

Growth doesn't happen in isolation, it happens in community.

And every reflective step strengthens your calm, your clarity and your confidence.

Chapter 8

# Interpersonal Skills

## STRENGTHENING YOUR INTERPERSONAL TOOLBOX

### Purpose

This reflection will help you examine how you currently communicate with your students and identify areas to refine your interpersonal approach.

Be honest. This is about awareness, not judgement.

Your interpersonal skills are often the difference between escalation and de-escalation, compliance and cooperation, resistance and rapport.

## SELF-AUDIT

Rate yourself from **1 (needs improvement)** to **5 (strong)** in the following areas.

| Interpersonal Skill | Rating (1–5) |
| --- | --- |
| I use a calm and appropriate tone of voice. | ____________ |
| I speak at eye level when addressing students. | ____________ |
| I actively listen without interrupting. | ____________ |
| I use open-ended questions to guide behaviour. | ____________ |
| I give clear, specific feedback (not just "good job"). | ____________ |

I use humour appropriately to connect with students.  __________

I respond to challenging behaviour without yelling or sarcasm.  __________

I acknowledge student feelings, even when I don't agree with them.  __________

**Total:**  ________ / 40

Are there any 3's or below? Those are powerful growth points.

Circle one area that would make the biggest difference in your classroom right now:

# PERSONAL REFLECTION

### Think of a Recent Escalation

Describe a recent moment when a behaviour incident escalated in your classroom.

What was said? What was your tone like? What did your body language communicate?

### Skill Check

Looking back, what interpersonal skill could have helped de-escalate that moment?

- Tone of voice

- Proximity

- Active listening

- Open-ended questioning

☐ Humour

☐ Specific feedback

☐ Emotional validation

☐ Neutral body language

Explain your thinking:

_______________________________________________

_______________________________________________

_______________________________________________

_______________________________________________

## Strengthening One Skill

What is one interpersonal skill you want to strengthen starting tomorrow?

Why is this the right focus area for you?

_______________________________________________

_______________________________________________

_______________________________________________

How will you intentionally practise this in your next lesson?

(Be specific – what will you say or do differently?)

# MICRO-PRACTICE PLAN

Complete the sentence:

"When a student challenges me, instead of ________________, I will ________________."

______________________________________________________

______________________________________________________

______________________________________________________

______________________________________________________

## Final Reflection

Strong interpersonal skills are not about being soft. They are about being steady.

The way you speak, stand, listen, and respond communicates more than your rules ever will.

Calm tone builds safety. Clear language builds respect. Intentional delivery builds authority.

Interpersonal mastery is a practice, not a personality trait.

What small shift will you commit to this week?

______________________________________________________

______________________________________________________

______________________________________________________

______________________________________________________

Chapter 9

# SCRIPT BANKS

## SCRIPT & LANGUAGE PRACTICE PAGES

Clear language reduces escalation. Predictable scripts build authority. Practised words create calm delivery.

These pages are designed to help you rehearse your responses before you need them.

## CALM REDIRECTION SCRIPTS

### Practise Neutral, Clear Language

Rewrite the reactive statement into a calm, professional response.

Reactive: "Stop it right now! I've had enough."

Calm Script:

___________________________________________________

Reactive: "Why do you always do this?"

Calm Script:

___________________________________________________

Reactive: "If you don't stop, you're in big trouble."

Calm Script:

___________________________________________________

Now create your own calm redirection phrase you can use consistently:

My Go-To Redirection Script:

_______________________________________________________________

_______________________________________________________________

_______________________________________________________________

## CONSEQUENCE DELIVERY PRACTICE

Complete the following scripts in your own voice.

"You're choosing to _____________________, which means _____________________."

_______________________________________________________________

"We agreed that when _______________ happens, the next step is _______________

_______________________________________________________________."

"I'm going to give you a moment to reset. When you're ready to _______________ _______________, you can rejoin us."

## OFFERING CHOICE (PREVENTING POWER STRUGGLES)

Offering structured choice keeps responsibility with the student.

Practise writing two-choice statements:

"You can choose to _________________________________, or you can choose to _____________________________."

Write one choice statement for a common behaviour in your classroom:

_______________________________________________________

_______________________________________________________

_______________________________________________________

# EMOTIONAL VALIDATION LANGUAGE

Acknowledging feelings does not mean excusing behaviour.

Complete the statements:

"I can see that you're feeling _________________________________."

"But the expectation is still _________________________________."

"I understand this is frustrating. What's a better choice you could make right now?"

Rewrite this in your own words:

_______________________________________________________

_______________________________________________________

_______________________________________________________

_______________________________________________________

# PRAISING THE RIGHT BEHAVIOUR

Specific praise strengthens behaviour.

Instead of: "Good job."

Try:

"I noticed you _________________________. That shows _________________________."

Write two specific praise statements you can use this week:

1. _________________________________________________

_________________________________________________

2. _________________________________________________

_________________________________________________

# MICRO-REHEARSAL

Choose one challenging scenario you commonly face.

Scenario:

_________________________________________________

Write your full calm response from start to finish:

_________________________________________________

_________________________________________________

# Final Reminder

You do not rise to the occasion in the moment.
You fall to the level of your preparation.

The more you rehearse calm scripts, the
more confidently you will deliver them when it
matters most.

**Practised language
becomes natural language.**

## Chapter 10

# CRACR TEMPLATES

**CRACR CLASSROOM**
**SCRIPT BANK**
Calm Language for Confident Teachers

A teacher's tone sets the room — use these scripts to maintain clarity, authority, and rapport.

- **Offering Structured Choice (prevents power struggles)**

  "You can choose to work with the group, or choose to work independently." "You can start now, or you can use your break time." "It's your decision. I know you can make a good one."

- **Naming the Choice**

  "You're choosing to ignore the expectation." "Right now, you're choosing disruption."
  "You have a choice here." "What's a better choice you could make?"

- **Delivering a Consequence**

  "We agreed that when this happens, this is the next step." "This is your first reminder." "You'll need to move seats so others can learn." "Take 2 minutes to reset and then rejoin us." "You can re-enter when you're ready to follow the expectation."

- **Emotional Validation**

  "I can see you're frustrated." "I understand you're upset." "It's okay to feel angry. It's not okay to disrupt learning." "Take a breath. We'll solve this calmly."

- **Restoring After Escalation**

  "Thankyou for resetting." "I appreciate you getting back on track." "Let's move forward." "We all make mistakes. What matters is what we do next."

- **Specific Praise That Builds Behaviour**

  Instead of "Good Job," try: "I noticed you raised your hand, which shows self-control" "You stayed focused, even when it was hard." "You made a better choice that time."

**adömsense**

# CRACR CLASSROOM SCRIPT BANK

# Calm Language for Confident Teachers

Remember, your tone sets the temperature of the room.
This script will help you maintain clarity, authority, and rapport.

## Calm Redirection

Instead of reacting emotionally, try:

- "Pause. Let's reset."

- "That's not our agreement."

- "Try that again the right way."

- "I'll wait."

- "We're not doing that here."

- "Check yourself."

## Naming the Choice

- "You're choosing to ignore the expectation."

- "Right now, you're choosing disruption."

- "You have a choice here."

- "What's a better choice you could make?"

# Delivering a Consequence

- "We agreed that when this happens, this is the next step."

- "This is your first reminder."

- "You'll need to move seats so others can learn."

- "Take two minutes to reset and then rejoin us."

- "You can re-enter when you're ready to follow the expectation."

# Offering Structured Choice (Prevents Power Struggles)

- "You can choose to work with the group or choose to work independently."

- "You can start now, or you can use your break time."

- "It's your decision. I know you can make a good one."

# Emotional Validation Without Excusing Behaviour

- "I can see you're frustrated."

- "I understand you're upset."

- "It's okay to feel angry. It's not okay to disrupt learning."

- "Take a breath. We'll solve this calmly."

# Restoring After Escalation

- "Thank you for resetting."

- "I appreciate you getting back on track."

- "Let's move forward."

- "We all make mistakes. What matters is what we do next."

# Specific Praise That Builds Behaviour

Instead of "Good job," try:

- I noticed you raised your hand, which shows self-control.

- "You stayed focused, even when it was hard."

- "You made a better choice that time."

- "That's leadership."

## Remember

Speak slowly.

Lower your voice.

Mean what you say.

Follow through.

Clarity reduces chaos.

Consistency builds trust.

**Scan QR code for printable posters.**

# DE-ESCALATION SCRIPT BANK

When emotions rise, reasoning drops. Your tone must be regulated before your words instruct

## When a student is escalating

- "Pause, lets take a breath."
- "I can see you're upset."
- "I'm here to help, not argue."

## Naming the Emotion

- "You look frustrated."
- "It seems like something didn't feel fair."
- "That felt disappointing."

## Creating Psychological Space 

- "Let's step over here."
- "Take two minutes."
- "You can rejoin when you're ready."

## Avoiding Power Struggles

- "You have two choices."
- "It's your decision."
- "I know you can make a better choice."
- "We agreed on the next step."

## After the Peak (re-entry language)

- "Are you ready to try again?"
- "Thank you for calming your body."
- "Lets move forward."
- "What would help you to do better next time?"

## Protecting Rapport During Consequences

- "This is about the behaviour, not you."
- "You're capable of better choices."
- "I still care about you."
- "We'll start fresh next lesson."

## For "Unicorn" Students (H.I.B)

- "I'm staying calm."
- "We'll talk when we're both calm."
- "You're safe here."

## What NOT to Say During Lines:

AVOID:

1. "Calm down!"
2. "What's wrong with you?"
3. "You're being ridiculous"
4. "You always ......"

**adomsense**

# DE-ESCALATION SCRIPT BANK

## Use Calm Language for Heated Moments

When emotions rise, reasoning drops.
Your tone must regulate before your words instruct.

Speak slowly. Lower your voice. Reduce your words.

# When a Student Is Escalating

- "Pause. Let's take a breath."

- "I can see you're upset."

- "We're going to slow this down."

- "I'm here to help, not argue."

- "Let's reset."

# Naming the Emotion (Without Fuelling It)

- "You look frustrated."

- "It seems like something didn't feel fair."

- "You're angry right now."

- "That felt disappointing."

Then follow with:

- "We'll solve it calmly."

- "We can talk once we're steady."

# Creating Psychological Space

- "Let's step over here."

- "Take two minutes."

- "You can rejoin when you're ready."

- "I'll give you space to reset."

# Avoiding Power Struggles

Instead of: "Do it now."
Try:

- "You have two choices."

- "It's your decision."

- "I know you can make a better choice."

- "We agreed on the next step."

# When a Student Refuses

- "I'm not going to argue."

- "This is the expectation."

- "You can choose to follow it now, or we follow the next step."

- "I'll wait."

# After the Peak (Re-Entry Language)

- "Are you ready to try again?"

- "Thank you for calming your body."

- "Let's move forward."

- "What would help you do better next time?"

# Protecting Rapport During Consequences

- "This is about the behaviour, not you."

- "You're capable of better choices."

- "I still care about you."

- "We'll start fresh next lesson."

# For "Unicorn" Students (High-Intensity Behaviour)

- "I'm staying calm."

- "I won't match your volume."

- "We'll talk when we're both regulated."

- "You're safe here."

# What NOT to Say During Escalation

Avoid:

- "Calm down!"

- "What's wrong with you?"

- "You're being ridiculous."

- "This is embarrassing."

- "You always…"

**Escalation feeds on emotion.**

**Neutrality drains it.**

# BEHAVIOUR BREAKDOWN TEMPLATE

## Analysing Real Classroom Incidents

Use this template after a challenging behaviour incident.
Keep it factual. Keep it reflective. Keep it honest.

This is not about blame. It is about insight.

**BEHAVIOUR BREAKDOWN TEMPLATE**

**Analysing Real Classroom Incidents**

Use this template after a challenging behaviour incident.
Keep it factual. Keep it reflective. Keep it honest.
This is not about blame. It is about insight.

### What Happened?

Describe the situation objectively.

- What was the behaviour?
- Who was involved?
- What was happening before it occurred?
- What was the immediate outcome?

### What Was the Likely Function Behind the Behaviour?

What was the student trying to gain or avoid?

☐ Attention
☐ Avoidance of the task
☐ Escape from a situation
☐ Sensory need
☐ Peer approval
☐ Power/control
☐ Emotional dysregulation
☐ Skill deficit
☐ Other: _______________________________

**Explain your thinking:**

### What Was My Response?

Be honest and specific.

- What did I say?
- What was my tone like?

**Scan QR code for printable posters.**

- What consequence (if any) was applied?
- Did I stay calm and consistent?

## Which Element of CRACR Did My Response Align With?

Reflect on your framework:

☐ C – Caring
☐ R – Rapport (Did I protect the relationship?)
☐ A – Applying Boundaries (Were my boundaries clear?)
☐ C – Consequence (Was it logical and consistent?)
☐ R – Reflection (Did I pause and evaluate?)

**Explain how your response aligned, or didn't:**

## What Will I Do Differently Next Time?

Focus on growth, not guilt.

- What could I adjust in my language?
- What boundary needs strengthening?
- What support might this student need?
- What will I practise before the next similar moment?

## Final Reset Statement

Complete this sentence:

"Next time this behaviour occurs, I will _________________________________
because _________________________________________________________."

### Reminder

Every behaviour is communication.
Every response is modelling.
Every incident is feedback.
Calm analysis today creates stronger leadership tomorrow.

# Reminder

**Every behaviour is communication.
Every response is modelling.
Every incident is feedback.**

**Calm analysis today creates
stronger leadership tomorrow.**

# IN-THE-MOMENT RESET CARD

**(For Escalating Behaviour)**

**Scan QR code for printable posters.**

## IN-THE-MOMENT RESET CARD
### FOR ESCALATING BEHAVIOUR

- Pause First - Ask yourself, Am I responding or reacting?
- Check your delivery - The calmest person holds the authority
- Return to the expectation- No lecture, no emotion, no debate.
- Offer structured choice - Keep responsibility with the student.
- Avoid the power struggle. Don't argue, raise volume or personalise.
- Protect rapport - This is about the behaviour, not you.
- Plan Re-entry - Say "Let's move forward"

### Remember
Fewer words. Lower voice. Slower pace.
Clear boundary

AFTERWARD - WAS I CONSISTENT? DID I STAY ALIGNED WITH CRACR? WHAT WILL I CHANGE NEXT TIME?

# Remember to:

## 1.    PAUSE FIRST

- Stop talking

- Breathe in for 4, out for 4

- Lower your voice

- Relax shoulders

**Ask yourself:**
Am I responding or reacting?

## 2.    CHECK YOUR DELIVERY

- Slow pace

- Neutral tone

- Minimal words

- Calm body language

**Remember:**
The calmest person holds the authority.

## 3.    RETURN TO THE EXPECTATION

Say:

"We agreed that when _______________ happens,

the next step is_______________."

No lecture.
No emotion.
No debate.

## 4.   OFFER STRUCTURED CHOICE

"You can choose to _______________ , or choose to _______________ ."

"It's your decision."

Keep responsibility with the student.

## 5. AVOID THE POWER STRUGGLE

If they resist:

- Do not argue

- Do not raise volume

- Do not personalise

- Say:
  "I'll wait."

## 6. PROTECT RAPPORT

"This is about the behaviour, not you."

"You're capable of better choices."

## 7. PLAN RE-ENTRY

"Thank you for resetting."

"Let's move forward."

# MICRO-RESET (Internal Script)

**"Slow down. Stay steady. Model calm."**

## AFTERWARD (Quick Check)

- Was I consistent?

- Did I stay aligned with CRACR?

- What will I adjust next time?

# Remember

**Fewer words.**
**Lower voice.**
**Slower pace.**
**Clear boundary.**


**Calm is contagious.**
**Consistency builds trust.**

# CRACR PARENT CONVERSATION FRAMEWORK

**Structured. Calm. Professional.**

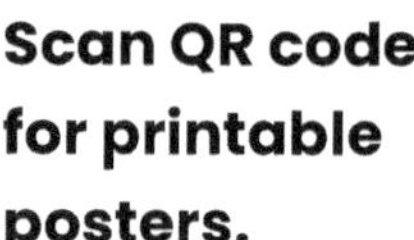

**Scan QR code for printable posters.**

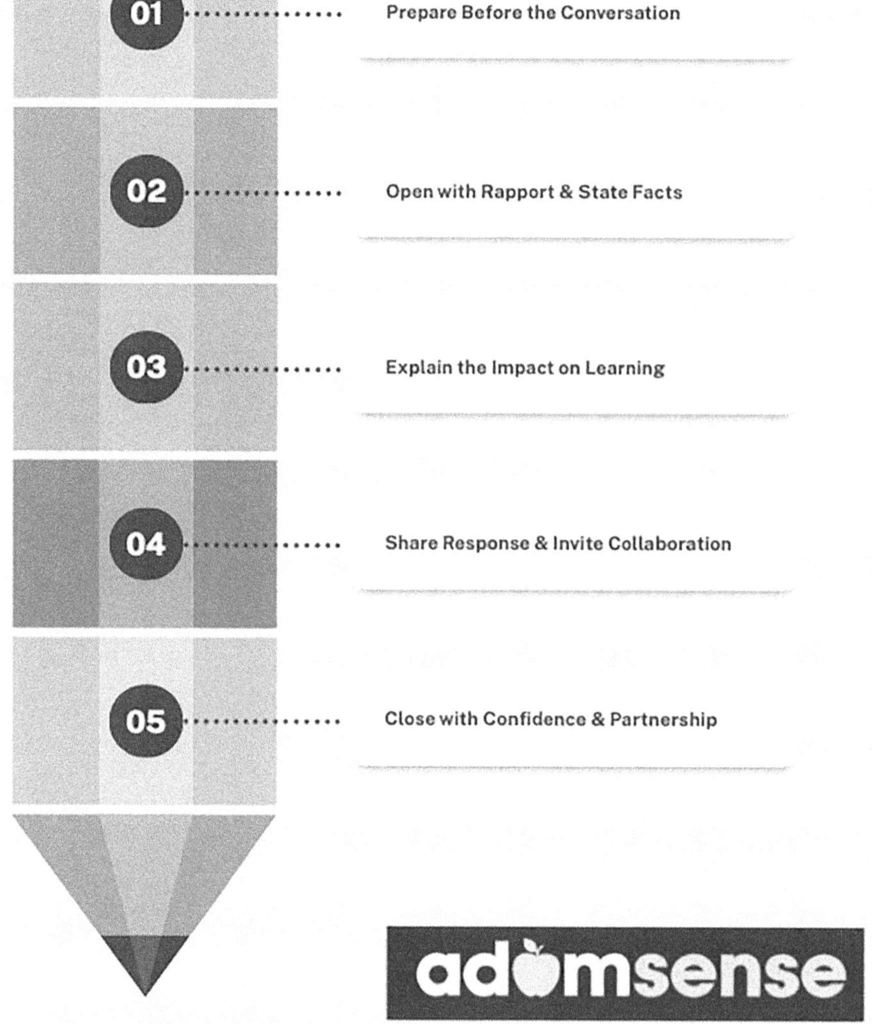

Parent conversations should never feel like a battlefield.

They are an opportunity to build alignment around one shared goal:

**The child's growth and success.**

Use this framework to stay steady, clear and collaborative.

# 1. PREPARE BEFORE THE CONVERSATION

Before calling or meeting:

- Clarify the behaviour (facts only)

- Identify the impact on learning

- Review your expectations and consequences

- Decide the outcome you're seeking

- Regulate yourself

Ask:

What is my intention - to blame or to partner?

# 2. OPEN WITH RAPPORT

Start with something genuine.

- "I enjoy having ___________________ in my class."

- "There are many strengths I see in your child."

- "I wanted to connect because I care about their progress."

This lowers defensiveness immediately.

# 3. STATE THE FACTS (NOT EMOTION)

Describe what happened without judgement.

Instead of:
"He was being disruptive."

Say:
"During independent work, he left his seat three times and called out across the room."

Stick to observable behaviour.

# 4.   EXPLAIN THE IMPACT

- "This made it difficult for others to concentrate."

- "It interrupted the flow of the lesson."

- "It prevented them from completing their work."

Parents need to understand why it matters.

# 5. SHARE THE RESPONSE

- "I gave a reminder."

- "We followed our agreed consequence."

- "He moved to a quiet desk to reset."

This shows consistency and professionalism.

# 6. INVITE COLLABORATION

- "Have you noticed anything similar at home?"

- "What strategies tend to work for you?"

- "How can we support him together?"

This shifts from confrontation to partnership.

# 7. CLOSE WITH CONFIDENCE

End positively and clearly.

- "I'm confident we can support him."

- "I'll keep you updated."

- "Thank you for working with me."

# SCRIPT EXAMPLES

### If a Parent Becomes Defensive

"I understand this is hard to hear. My intention isn't to criticise, it's to support your child."

### If a Parent Minimises the Behaviour

"I understand it may not seem significant, but in a classroom of 28 students, consistency is essential."

### If a Parent Blames the Teacher

"I'm sorry you feel this way. I'm always reflecting on my practice, and I'm also committed to maintaining clear expectations for all students."

### If a Parent Is Emotional

"I can hear how much you care. Let's work through this calmly together."

# What NOT To Do

**X**  Argue

**X**  Over-explain

**X**  Defend emotionally

**X**  Blame the child

**X**  Blame the parent

**Stay factual.**
**Stay steady.**
**Stay student-focused.**

## Final Reminder

**You are not there to win.**
**You are there to lead.**

**Professional tone builds trust.**
**Consistency builds credibility.**
**Clarity builds partnership.**

# CRACR REPAIR CONVERSATION TEMPLATE

## Restoring Relationship After a Behaviour Incident

### CRACR REPAIR CONVERSATION TEMPLATE

**HOW TO RESTORE A RELATIONSHIP AFTER A BEHAVIOUR INCIDENT**

Repair is not about revisiting the drama. It is about restoring dignity, accountability, and connection.

**adömsense**

Have repair conversations when: • The student is calm • You are regulated • The audience is gone • Learning time is not being interrupted.

**NEVER REPAIR IN THE HEAT OF THE MOMENT**

**1  START WITH SAFETY**
Lower the intensity immediately.
• "Let's talk for a minute."
• "This isn't about getting you in trouble."
• "I want to help you do better next time."
Tone: calm, steady, respectful.

**2  DESCRIBE THE BEHAVIOUR (FACTS ONLY)**
• "During group work, you called out several times."
• "You walked out when I gave instructions."
• "You used language that wasn't respectful."
Avoid: "You were rude." Stick to observable behaviour.

**3  INVITE REFLECTION:** "What was happening for you?" "What were you feeling?" "What were you hoping would happen?" Let them speak. Do not interrupt. Listen fully.

**4  CONNECT TO THE IMPACT:** "When that happened, others couldn't concentrate." "It disrupted the lesson." Keep it calm and matter of fact.

**5  RETURN TO ACCOUNTABILITY**
"What could you do differently next time?"
"What would a better choice look like?"
"How can you repair this?"
Encourage the student to generate the solution.

**6  RESTORE THE RELATIONSHIP & RE-ENTRY PLAN**
"I still care about you." "You're capable of better choices." "We're starting fresh."

**7**
"Next time you feel frustrated, what's your plan?"
Discipline teaches behaviour. Repair builds character.

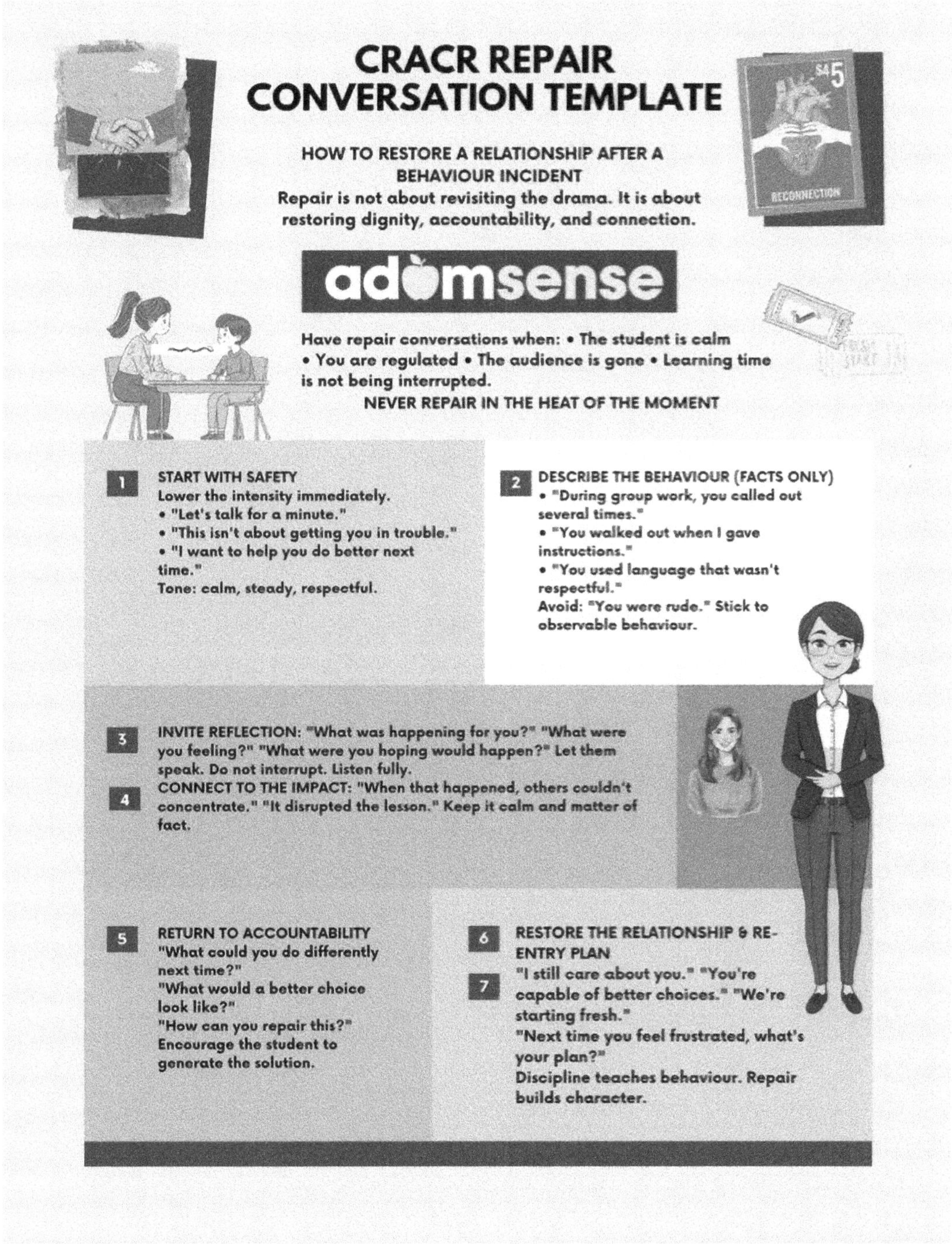

**Scan QR code for printable posters.**

Repair is not about revisiting the drama. It is about restoring dignity, accountability and connection.

Have repair conversations when:

- The student is calm
- You are regulated
- The audience is gone
- Learning time is not being interrupted

Never repair in the heat of the moment.

## 1. START WITH SAFETY

Lower the intensity immediately.

- "Let's talk for a minute."
- "This isn't about getting you in trouble."
- "I want to help you do better next time."

Tone: calm, steady, respectful.

## 2. DESCRIBE THE BEHAVIOUR (FACTS ONLY)

- "During group work, you called out several times."
- "You walked out when I gave instructions."
- "You used language that wasn't respectful."

Avoid:

- "You were rude."
- "You embarrassed me."
- "You always do this."

Stick to observable behaviour.

# 3. INVITE REFLECTION

- "What was happening for you?"

- "What were you feeling?"

- "What were you hoping would happen?"

Let them speak

Do not interrupt.

Listen fully.

# 4. CONNECT TO THE IMPACT

- "When that happened, others couldn't concentrate."

- "It disrupted the lesson."

- "It made it harder for you to complete your work."

Keep it calm and matter of fact.

# 5. RETURN TO ACCOUNTABILITY

- "What could you do differently next time?"

- "What would a better choice look like?"

- "How can you repair this?"

Encourage the student to generate the solution.

## 6. RESTORE THE RELATIONSHIP

- "I still care about you."

- "You're capable of better choices."

- "We're starting fresh."

This protects rapport.

## 7. RE-ENTRY PLAN

- "Next time you feel frustrated, what's your plan?"

- "If this happens again, what will you try first?"

Make it specific.

## QUICK SCRIPT FLOW

"I noticed ______________________.

What was happening for you?

When that happened, ______________________.

What's a better choice next time?

Let's reset."

# What Repair Is NOT

**X**    A lecture

**X**    A threat

**X**    A reminder of past mistakes

**X**    Public

**X**    Sarcastic

Repair is private, calm and forward-focused.

## Final Reminder 

**Discipline teaches behaviour.**
**Repair builds character.**

**The strongest authority figures are those
who correct and then reconnect.**

# ADAMSENSE PROFESSIONAL LEARNING

Adamsense provides research-informed, classroom-tested professional development aligned with the CRACR model.

**Services include:**

- **School-based workshops and implementation programs**

- **University teacher-education sessions**

- **Conference keynote presentations**

- **Behaviour and leadership consultancy**

Designed for real classrooms. Delivered with clarity. Built for sustainable change.

**Enquiries and bookings:**
Michele@adamsense.com
adamsenseteaching@gmail.com
Facebook: adamsense teaching
Instagram: adamsense.teaching
www.adamsense.com

## About the Author – Michele Adamson

Michele Adamson is a passionate educator, author and the founder of Adamsense, with over 20 years of experience working in primary schools across Queensland. Throughout her career, Michele has worked as a classroom teacher, relief teacher and behaviour specialist, supporting both students and teachers in some of the most challenging classroom environments.

But more than anything, Michele is someone who truly cares about people.

She has always been driven by a deep desire to help others succeed, not just academically but also emotionally and personally. Whether it's a student struggling to feel safe in the classroom or a teacher feeling overwhelmed and questioning their ability, Michele is the person who steps in, listens, and helps them find a way forward.

Her work alongside school psychologists and behaviour teams gave her a unique insight into the real challenges teachers face every day. She saw firsthand how many capable, caring educators were burning out; not because they didn't care enough, but because they didn't have a clear, practical framework to guide them through complex behaviour.

This is what led Michele to develop the C.R.A.C.R. model - a simple, structured approach designed to bring calm, clarity and confidence back into the classroom. It's not built on theory alone, but on real experiences, real classrooms and real conversations with teachers who needed support.

Michele is also the author of Adamsense: 10 Steps to Thrive in Teaching, a book created to help teachers regain balance, reduce overwhelm and rediscover the joy in their profession.

Outside of the classroom, Michele is a wife and mother, and understands the juggle that comes with balancing a demanding career and family life. This is why her work is grounded not only in effectiveness but in sustainability, helping teachers thrive both inside and outside the classroom.

Through her books, workshops and speaking, Michele's mission is simple: to help teachers move from surviving to thriving, and to remind them that they are not alone.

# Scan QR code to access Free Resources